The Invisible Me

T0116817

CAROL CAMPBELL-NORRIS

authorHOUSE®

AuthorHouse™
1663 Liberty Drive
Bloomington, IN 47403
www.authorhouse.com
Phone: 1-800-839-8640

Published by AuthorHouse   03/08/2012

ISBN: 978-1-4567-6059-5 (sc)
ISBN: 978-1-4567-6058-8 (e)

Library of Congress Control Number: 2011907432

Acknowledgment

This book is dedicated to my husband, Dohen, and my two daughters, Marisol and Monique. Also to Edna Francois and Elisa Fuentes, for your support, I show my deepest appreciation.

Table of Contents

Chapter 1

I Am the Invisible Me

And God said to Moses, "I Am Who I AM . . . .
The Lord God of your fathers, the God of
Abraham, the God of Isaac, and the God of Jacob,
has sent me to you. This is my name forever,
and this is My memorial to all generations"
(Exodus 3:14&15, NKJV).

How is it that Christians believe in a God they cannot see and are willing to pour out their hearts to someone who "never speaks back?" That, in itself, is a mystery to those who have never experienced the peace that comes from knowing Christ Jesus. It is strange that at times when you least expect it, prayers are answered and life is beautiful; yet, at other times life appears so chaotic and nothing you pray for seems to comes thru. You pray and you cry but the problem gets worse and you feel broken. However, with the Christian, whether times are bad or good, there is a constant peace that is felt in the inner-most part of the soul that exudes unexplainable joy. It gives the assurance that things are going to be alright, that God the Father is still in control, and that He is near even though, with natural eyes, He cannot be seen.

I remember waking up out of bed one morning and before I could even place my feet on the floor I began to cry out to God, "God help me!" I felt so broken and so alone. After all, this was a new day. I should be looking forward to what the day had to offer, but "no." Something in my spirit felt sad and alone. I needed assurance that this day, today, would be different than all the other days. I needed to feel that peace within along with the joy I already had in my heart from knowing Christ as my personal Savior.

Knowing that one day Jesus Christ would come back for me was just not enough. Life circumstances had taken a hold of me and my strength was almost gone. Like many, I worked so hard throughout life to get to the top of the ladder only to find myself without a job and starting all over again. "Father, God," I cried, "Please Lord, please help me to get my life in order. I have responsibilities, I have bills to pay, and I need to get out of debt. Please Lord, help me to find a job, or just even open a door for me so I can see that you are near."

I had poured out my heart and requested my needs to the God of the universe. I looked to Him to take care of me. He said, "Ask and it will be given to you; seek, and you will find; knock, and it will be opened to you" (Mathew 7:7, NKJV). When you think about it, it all comes down to trust. Do I trust Him to take care of me? Do I trust that He is capable of taking care of my needs? I believe, but do I trust. His word says, "For I know the thoughts that I think toward you, says the Lord, thoughts of peace and not of evil, to give you a future and a hope. Then you will call upon Me and go and pray to Me, and I will listen to you; and you will seek Me and find Me, when you search for Me with all your heart" (Jeremiah 29:11-13, NKJV). My responsibility as a child of God is to trust that He loves me more than I love myself and that whatever He plans for me, He is working it out for my own good. So I wait to hear from Him and though I cannot see Him, I know He is near and He knows that it is in Him that I place my trust.

When Abraham was told by God to leave his homeland, he took his family, not knowing where the Lord would lead him. He had to trust totally upon God for his direction. Nevertheless, as he journeyed, one could see how Abraham's trust at times waivered. Although Abraham would sometimes take matters into his own hands, God never left him. But let us not be too hard on Abraham; we are no better. To say we trust God is very easy, to put trust into action is when it becomes difficult. All throughout the written word we are reminded to trust in God. Both the Old and New Testament testify to the result of those who trust Him. Yet their trust did not come overnight. They had to be constantly refined by God to prove their faithfulness. Sarah, after being barren for so long, surely must have wondered where all these children that God promised her husband would come from. Didn't God say that He would give Abraham a great nation? But as usual, we take God's business into our own hands. "We must fix it because God is taking too long. Maybe He has forgotten us or maybe I did not hear His voice. It was all in my head." So Sarah gave Abraham her servant Hagar to be his wife. But as usual when we take matters into our own hands God has to come and fit the pieces together.

Twice Hagar was sent away from the house of Abraham. The first time Sarah sent her away for being disrespectful, but God saw Hagar's plight and came to her rescue. Think about it. Hagar was Sarah's servant. She never asked to be the wife of her master. She had no say in the matter. Now that she had become Abraham's mistress, of course she would now feel that she should share some of the same privileges as Sarah. Nevertheless, Hagar must have known the God of Abraham, because as soon as the angel told her of her future she was willing to obey and trust in the word of God. Hagar called the name of the Lord who spoke to her, "You are the God who Sees" for she said, "Have I also here seen Him who sees me?" (Genesis 16:13, NKJV).

The second time Hagar was sent away, Sarah, because of her concern about race and position, asked Abraham to remove Hagar along with her son Ishmael from their camp. Hagar was an Egyptian woman and a slave. Of course, she was not good enough to be a part of their family now that Sarah had bore her own child Isaac, who was a pure descendant. One could see conflict at every angle since Ishmael was the first son for Abraham, and Isaac followed. Not to mention, Ishmael lived with

Abraham for a long time before Isaac came on the scene which meant they had already bonded and had formed a very close relationship.

How hard it must have been for Abraham to do what his wife Sarah had asked. But again God always shows up to fix the mess we get ourselves in when we fail to trust him. In Abraham's grief God told Abraham to do what Sarah had asked and reminded him of the promise He had made. God told Abraham that out of Ishmael there would be a great nation because Ishmael was his seed. God was merciful to Hagar and brought comfort to her as she cried out to Him about her predicament. God had removed all fear from Hagar as she was reminded also of the promise He had made to make Ishmael a great nation.

Throughout the Bible there are experiences that help us to see the magnitude of God and His love for the human race, yet if we do not know Him for ourselves we will never learn how to trust Him. After all, how can you trust a God that you have never met but only heard about? God spoke to Moses out of the fire. He has never showed His face because no man has ever seen God and lived. Moses is the only man that has ever come very close to seeing God. He saw the hands of God as He wrote the Ten Commandments for the children of Israel, and the shadow of God, which caused Moses hair to become white and his countenance to glow. In case anyone makes the mistake to say they have seen the face of God, Moses warned: "Take careful heed to yourselves, for you saw no form when the Lord spoke to you at Horeb out of the midst of the fire, lest you act corruptly and make yourselves a carved image in the form of any figure: the likeness of male or female, the likeness of any animal that is on the earth or the likeness of any winged bird that flies in the air, the likeness of anything that creeps on the ground or the likeness of any fish that is in the water beneath the earth. And take heed, lest you lift your eyes to Heaven, and when you see the sun, the moon, and the stars, all the host of Heaven, you feel driven to worship them and serve them, which the Lord your God has given to all peoples under the whole Heaven as a heritage" (Deuteronomy 4 :15-19, NKJV).

The Angel of the Lord first appeared to Moses in the form of a burning bush. His curiosity got a hold of him and he drew closer. God then called out of the burning bush to him and he answered, "Here I am." God warned him not to come any closer but to remove his shoes from his feet for the place where he stood was holy ground. I can only imagine the fear and joy that went through the heart of Moses as he heard the voice of God. As God instructed Moses about what He wanted him to do, Moses may have wondered if what was happening to him was real and would anybody believe that he actually talked to God.

Certainly, he wanted to obey God's instructions; however, there was a huge BUT. Who is God? What is your name? God answered, "I Am Who I Am." And He said, "Thus you shall say to the children of Israel, 'I AM has sent me to you'" (Exodus 3:14, NKJV). More clearly, Tell Israel "I AM" has sent you. Let us not mistake ourselves in believing that God is invisible. Jesus Christ Himself, when He addressed the Pharisees also bore witness, that God is His Father and that He had sent Him to be a witness, that God is in the midst of our lives, and that the Father cares about us. Jesus said, "I am One who bears witness of Myself, and the Father who sent Me bears witness of Me" (John 8:18 NKJV). Jesus further stated, "You are from beneath; I am from above. You are of this world; I am not of this world" (John 8:23 NKJV); and "Most assuredly, I say to you, before Abraham was, I AM" (John 8:58, NKJV). God loved us so much and wanted us to know how He missed being close to us, so He sent His own son, Jesus Christ to come on His behalf. Yet they abused Him, mocked Him, and treated Him less than a human being. No matter how Jesus pleaded with them to understand that He was the Christ sent from God they could not comprehend. Jesus even asked them to believe Him for the very works they had seen Him perform but still they rejected Him. After all, His coming was written by the very prophets in whom they believed yet they still denied Him.

Jesus could not lie and would not lie to save His life for He knew for sure where He had came from and who had sent Him. Today, some still deny the very existence of Christ, more so the Father. Let us not be deceived. Jesus also said "I and My Father are one." (John 10:30, NKJV). It's been over two thousand years since Jesus physically walked on this earth and some may have become weary or absent minded about God's existence. We may not be able to see His face or hold His hands but we all can feel that we are connected to someone bigger than ourselves. We sometimes cannot explain it, but we certainly believe it. For He continuously moves in our lives. Every breath we take is by the power of the Invisible God.

Personal Reflection

_____

_____

_____

_____

_____

_____

_____

_____

_____

_____

_____

_____

_____

_____

_____

_____

_____

_____

_____

_____

_____

_____

Chapter 2

I Know the Desires of Your Heart

.... "For the Lord does not see as man sees;
for man looks at the outward appearance,
but the Lord looks at the heart"
(1 Samuel 16: 7, NKJV).

Isn't it absurd how we tell the Lord what we want Him do in our lives to make it better, as if we know what is best for us and He doesn't? Think about it. When we pray and ask God to bless us, we already determine what our blessings should look like in our minds. Some of us envision it to be a nice car, a big house, to be top-ranked in all of our classes, to be debt free, or maybe, that big promotion on the job. We rarely think of blessings as being able to breathe or having our loved ones near us. Our daily survival is a blessing in itself. Most of us enjoy the mere fact of having a place to sleep, food to eat, and clothes to wear without even thinking about those who do not possess these things. Still God with His infinite grace provides for us daily. He is with us every step of the way. With each breath we take, know that the God of Abraham, Isaac and Jacob cares for you and for me. Peter encourages us in his words, "Therefore humble yourselves under the mighty hand of God, that He may exalt you in due time, casting all your care upon Him, for He cares for you (1 Peter 5:6&7, NKJV).

I am touched with the news of tragedies and catastrophes that happen all over the world. I think about children who have lost their parents, the elderly and the widow, who have to struggle to make ends meet. Yes, I am touched by the teenager who is being molested by a family member, or the father who is heart-broken because he can't find a job to provide for his children. I am truly touched. In my humanity I sometimes ask God "why?" "Why is there so much suffering? Why all this hatred and war? Why Lord?" Then the answer comes to me loud and clear, "It is Because of Sin". Our disobedience to God has created havoc in our homes, churches, our schools, our communities, and our society. The world is gone beyond fixing, for sin has taken its roots in the deepest part of its core. Even those who know God and trust in His words are also affected by the sins of the world. Yet, though we were all born in sin and shaped in iniquity, still it pleased the Lord to call us His own.

When Adam and Eve sinned, He had to put them out of the Garden of Eden but He never forgot about them. He was still a part of their lives. Yes, His heart was broken for He knew what was ahead for mankind. He taught them how to survive and what they needed to do in order to possess eternal life for man's death was imminent. Consider God's love when we observe the situation between Cain who killed his brother Abel. God came to Cain and asked for his brother even though He knew all things. For God asked, "What have you done? The voice of your brother's blood cries out to Me from the ground" (Genesis 4:10, NKJV). Cain was disobedient to God's instruction; therefore, his offering to God was not accepted. What created more of an impact for me was the fact that God knew Cain so well. God knew what was in Cain's heart and what lay ahead for him so God warned Cain. For the Lord also asked Cain, "Why are you angry? And why has your countenance fallen? If you do well, will you not be accepted? And if you do not do well, sin lies at the door. And its desire is for you, but you should rule over it" (Genesis 4:6&7, NKJV). Nevertheless, Cain succumbed to sin and finally killed his brother.

Let us examine some of the things that might have entered Cain's heart for him to develop such anger towards his brother Abel. Firstly, we know Cain was disobedient because God was not pleased with his offering. So God must have asked for something specific from both Cain and Abel. Secondly, Cain became jealous, which is to say, he had resentment in his heart for his brother, and he was envious. Imagine the dept of Cain's jealousy for it to have led him to such anger. Cain must have hated Abel so much to give that final blow that brings Abel to his death. When sin enters your heart, you never know what you will end up doing. You just can't trust yourself without God's power. God advises us to take control over sin, which means we have a choice whether to let sin control our lives and lead us to damnation, or we can submit ourselves to God who will give us power to overcome sin and be lead to victory in Jesus Christ.

God is always ready to forgive when we mess up. Cain did wrong when he killed his brother and committed the first murder. Think about it for one moment. This was the very first time in God's creation that a human being was murdered. The God who gave life must have been devastated to see what sin had done to His world. As Cain pleaded for mercy, he said, "My punishment is greater than I can bear! Surely You have driven me out this day from the face of the ground; I shall be hidden from Your face; I shall be a fugitive and a vagabond on the earth, and it will happen that anyone who finds me will kill me" (Genesis 4:13&14, NKJV). Yet, God was ready to offer Cain love and redemption. God showed Cain mercy in his sin. For God assured Cain that no one would kill him for He had made it a declaration stating, "Whoever kills Cain, vengeance shall be taken on him sevenfold" (Genesis 4:15, NKJV). Then the Lord went further to protect Cain by putting a mark on him so no one would make the mistake of saying, "I did not know it was him." Cain had a deceitful heart towards his brother. Eventually what lay in

Cain's heart was made visible in his action towards his brother Abel.

How can we then determine the desires of someone's heart, when we cannot determine their true intentions? We may see a smile but we don't know if there is hurt or pain beneath the surface. There are so many people who are hurting in this world but are afraid to express their heart. There are also people whose heart is constantly filled with evil and we still may not know. The Lord reminds us to be aware of wolves in sheep clothing. God is the only one that truly knows what goes on in the hearts of men and He alone can determine man's desires. He knows our needs and He knows our wants. He knows whether we have love in our hearts or whether we have hate. He knows if we are driven to do good or to do evil. Therefore, it is not for us to judge what goes on in people's hearts. Our concern is to take care of our own hearts, making sure our heart is what God desires it to be. When we are full of God's love, our hearts will extend to those who are hurting and in pain and they will feel the love of Christ through us. Our obligation concerning the hearts of men is to point them towards Christ through His love and He will do the rest. We cannot save anyone, only Jesus can, for He alone gave His life on the cross for our sins.

How loved Cain must have felt when God showed him mercy. "For the wages of sin is death, but the gift of God is eternal life in Christ Jesus our Lord" (Romans 6:23, NKJV). Jesus knows your hurt and what you are going through. Sometimes we can't even express ourselves, but He hears and understands. Whatever your problem is, He asked for you to bring it to Him. You may take your problem to a friend but your friend can only listen and give advice. It is always good to be encouraged by a friend but God knows your deepest thoughts and desires and He is working out everything for your good. So don't be afraid, victory is on its way. God has the power to stop your secret love affair. He has the power to meet your bills and stop the creditors from calling. He has the power to heal your ailing body, and cure an incurable disease. He has the power to ease your troubled mind.

Therefore, when life is not what you desire it to be and though at times you may go through great tribulations, keep trusting. For He knows your desires before you can even fathom them yourself. God knows about you and sees ahead into your future. Be faithful and cling to His words. "Fear not, for I am with you. Be not dismayed, for I am your God. I will strengthen you, yes I will help you; I will uphold you with my righteous right hand" (Isaiah

41: 10, NKJV). All He asks is that you stay obedient to His word. "Trust in the Lord, and do good. Dwell in the land, and feed on His faithfulness. Delight yourself also in the Lord, and He shall give you the desires of your heart" (Psalm 37: 3 &4, NKJV).

Personal Reflection

Chapter 3

What Has Separated You from Me

Then the serpent said to the woman,
"You will not surely die"
(Genesis 3:4, NKJV).

As I thought about the goodness of God and His awesomeness, it dawned on me that the God who created the universe, and made man in His own image has engraved His signature on everything including the things that are seen and unseen. God knows everything about us and our world. He knew us before our parents thought of coming together. Think about it. God knew our names before it was even considered as a thought by the one who named us. There is nothing under the earth or beneath the sun or above the Heavens that can be hidden from Him who spoke all things into existence.

The Bible depicts the story of Sarah being promised to have a son (Geneses 18). Abraham and Sarah were old; as a result, Sarah had passed the age of child bearing. However, Sarah had overheard the conversation between her husband, Abraham, and the Angel of the Lord saying, she would have a son in her old age. Sarah laughed in her heart and doubted that even such a thing would happen seeing she had passed the age of bearing a child. Let's be honest with ourselves. If you were in Sarah's position wouldn't you have laughed as well? Many still doubt ever getting married because they waited for years for Mr. Right. You may have even doubted the plans

God has for your life and have fought against doing the will of God because of fear.

Sarah did not laugh openly but laughed in her heart. So when the angel of the Lord asked Sarah why she laughed, Sarah said, "I did not laugh". But the Angel of the Lord concluded the conversation by saying, "Yes you did". I feel that right away Sarah knew in her heart that this promise would become a reality. Even if at first she did not have enough faith to believe, the very fact that the angel of the Lord revealed her thoughts inspired her belief.

God is in touch with us and He knows what goes on in our day to day lives. He knows our future and He knows our past. Therefore, what can separate us from Him? What would cause God not to be near? As I pondered the question in my mind, I thought about the many times that I felt far from God. Time after time I would pray and feel as if God had left me for my problems seemed unbearable. At times my faith would waiver and sometimes I would contemplate my life and the struggles that I go through from time to time.

Let us examine the first time man was ever separated from God. The Lord God commanded man, saying, "Of every tree of the garden you may freely eat; but of the tree of the knowledge of good and evil you shall not eat, for in the day that you eat of it you shall surely die" (Geneses 2: 16 &17, NKJV). When Adam and Eve chose to disobey God, they chose to separate themselves from Him. Adam and Eve were no longer innocent. They now acquired the knowledge of what was good and evil for they had eaten of the forbidden fruit. Sin, through disobedience, came over the whole earth and man was separated from God.

You and I have to understand. God is so pure sin cannot exist in His presence. Remember God use to fellowship with Adam and Eve in the Garden. But as "they heard the sound of the Lord God walking in the garden in the cool of the day, Adam and his wife hid themselves from the present of the Lord God among the trees of the garden(Geneses 3:8, NKJV). Adam and Eve were not innocent anymore. They had the right to choose to do good or evil. It seems as if, from the beginning, man has always been fascinated by the unknown. If the serpent did not introduce the unknown to Eve we might have all been living in the Garden of Eden right now. As sin continued to increase on the earth God became more distant. Because of Adam and Eve's sin we too continue to make excuses to God and man for our own disobedience.

When Jesus was in the garden of Gethsemane praying for God to take away the cup which He was about to receive, He prayed, "O My Father, if it is possible, let this cup pass from Me; nevertheless, not as I will, but as You will" (Matthew 26:42, NKJV). Jesus knew that ultimately His dying on the cross would totally redeem man from sin. Man would be able to talk to God for himself and there would be no need for a priest for Jesus Himself would be the priest for all. Whether we are rich or poor, young or old, educated or uneducated, Jews or Gentiles, Black or White, Jesus carried all of our sins to the cross and became the final sacrifice for all.

Jesus became a sin offering for us although He never sinned. All our sins were laid on Him. God made the ultimate sacrifices to prove His love for us. He gave His only son Jesus Christ to become a sacrifice in our place. God was so broken. He had to turn away His face from man's cruelty towards Jesus His son. Remember, Jesus cried out to His Father, "My God, My God, why have You forsaken Me?" (Matthew 27:46, NKJV). Even the son of God felt separated from His Father. It is said, when Jesus was on the cross He felt all alone and alienated from God. Darkness covered the earth for three hours. "Then the sun was darkened, and the veil of the temple was torn in two. And when Jesus had cried out with a loud voice, He said, 'Father into your hands I commit My spirit.' Having said this, He breathed

His last" (Luke 23:44-46, NKJV). I am convinced that God must have hurt so much to see His son on the cross, that in those few hours He turned away His face, darkness covered the earth. I believe at that very moment Jesus felt the presence of His father and knew that His work had ended, the victory was almost won. The hardest part was over.

When I am at my lowest moment in life, it is when I remember Christ's death on the cross I am consoled that I am not alone. For even Jesus the son of God felt alone as well. God was willing to sacrifice His son for me so I could be reclaimed into His kingdom. I don't have to be overcome with my problems for God made provision through Jesus Christ to give me strength to go on. "Who shall separate us from the love of Christ? Shall tribulation, or distress, or persecution, or famine, or nakedness, or peril, or sword? As it is written; *'for Your sake we are killed all day long; We are accounted as sheep for the slaughter.'* Yet in all these things we are more than conquerors through Him who loved us. For I am persuaded that neither death nor life, nor angels nor principalities nor powers, nor things present nor things to come, nor height nor depth, nor any other created thing, shall be able to separate us from the love of God which is in Christ Jesus our Lord" (Romans 8:35-39, NKJV).

Let us cleave to these words and be encouraged in our faith. God hates when we sin but He loves us. He separates Himself from our sins but never from us for we are covered by the blood of Jesus Christ our lord and Savior.

Personal Reflection

_____

_____

_____

_____

_____

_____

_____

_____

_____

_____

_____

_____

_____

_____

_____

_____

_____

_____

_____

_____

_____

_____

_____

Chapter 4

One Thing I Require of You

"If you love Me, keep My commandments"
(John 14:15, NKJV).

When I reflect on my times of despair, I realize those were the times I felt far from God. It was as though my prayers never left the room and I felt far from Him. Nothing ever seemed to go right and my heart would become overwhelmed with hopelessness. At times the Holy Spirit would speak to my heart and remind me of whom I am. Have you ever had that experience of feeling far from God? There is no reason to feel ashamed and admit these feelings because life is real and our feelings are real.

I want you to understand that when God made us He equipped us with everything we would need to stay connected to Him. Remember the whole reason for man's creation is that we would worship God. We were made for His pleasure. Man was made for God by God. Yet we go about our business as if we exist only for ourselves. We have to be honest with ourselves in order for God to convict us. We sometimes feel like we are better than others and therefore act as if we are. How little do we forget that it is but for the grace of God why we are able to move, communicate, hold down a job or even breathe. Yet we chose to forget that He who made us would know what is best for us. That is just common sense. If your car breaks down would you go to a Plummer to get it fix? It would be ridiculous not to take it to a mechanic. However, we tend to treat God as if He is an after thought. "Oh I have tried everything and it has not worked so let me try Jesus".

Don't think that I am trying to point a finger because I am the chief of sinners. Yes, remember my feelings of despair, well that's what happens to me when I leave God out of my life. It is as though I put Him up on a shelf to be used at my own convenience. I love God and I adore Him, but please don't mess with my plans. I have everything under control! Just give me your blessings. Before long my life would turn upside down. I would then pour out my heart to Him, and He in His mercy and grace forgives me, and helps me to take up the pieces. God requires one thing from us and that is to be obedient. Through His word He instructs us to follow His commandments. Jesus said, "If you love Me keep my commandments" (John 14:15, NKJV).

When God destroyed the earth of evil men with the flood, God's desire was for man to turn from evil and come to know and love Him again. But as the earth multiplied with people they reverted back to evil. He yearned for a people who would love righteousness rather than evil. He wanted to teach man what it meant to live upright and just and how to abstain from sin. So God looked at all the nations of the earth to fine a good man. God wanted to rise up a holy nation, a peculiar people and He found Abraham. God's hand picked Abraham because He had watched him and knew the desires of his heart. Abraham was tested and tried and he passed the test of obedience. Remember, Abraham's greatest test was to prove his fear for God. Abraham had to sacrifice his beloved son. He had sent away Ishmael, the son he had with the Egyptian woman, and it had broken his heart. Now he was left with the only son he had with Sarah—the true lineage. Remember also that both Abraham and Sarah were considered elderly at the time so it was not likely that they had plans to have many more children. Sarah being able to give birth was a miracle within itself, a promise fulfilled by God. Yet Abraham was obedient to God and was willing to carry out His wishes.

I can imagine how Abraham's heart broke as he got closer and closer to where he would sacrifice his son. How would he go on with the memories of Isaac's laughter, his boyish play and the joy that captivates his heart every time he hears him say, "Father, I love you?" Yes, that must have been the longest and the most difficult journey for Abraham, yet he remained obedient. He must have contemplated what he would tell Sarah, but then again, Sarah knew God and the status of God. Did God not reveal Himself to her as well? She did have a child in her old age just as it was promised. She did struggle in her heart and was rebuked by the servant of the Lord who read her thoughts. Sarah knew God and what He required. Abraham would just have to trust God to comfort Sarah as she would later grieve her son.

As Isaac and Abraham got closer to the place where the sacrifice was to take place, Isaac helped his father to prepare for the sacrifice, still there was no lamb. Isaac asked, Father where is the lamb for the burnt offering and Abraham answered, God will provide. What amazes me most was the fact that Isaac did not run away when he found out that he was to be the sacrificial offering. The Bible said he was bound by his father and laid on the altar. "And Abraham stretched out his hand and took the knife to slay his son. But the angel of the Lord called to him from Heaven and said, 'Abraham, Abraham!' So he said, 'Here I am.' And He said, 'Do not lay your hand on the lad, or do anything to him; for now I know that you fear God, since you have not withheld your son, your only son, from Me.'"(Genesis 22: 10, 11&12, NKJV).

God prepared a lamb and the boy's life was spared. Abraham had passed the test. He proved He loved the Lord and that he was obedient and God blessed him. For God said to Abraham, "By Myself I have sworn, because you have done this thing, and have not withheld your son, your only son, blessing I will bless you and multiplying I will multiply your descendants as the stars of the Heaven and as the sand which is on the seashore; and your descendants shall possess the gate of their enemies. In your seed all the nations of the earth shall be blessed, because you have obeyed My voice" (Geneses 22: 16-18, NKJV).

Because of one man's obedience a whole nation was blessed. This reminds me of the sacrifice God made as well. What I love about God is that He does not ask us to do something that he would not do Himself for us. Abraham proved himself to God and God proved Himself to us when He gave His only son Jesus Christ to become a human sacrifice for us. Remember we are made in the image of God and so we carry all the emotions known to God. So in case you forget God also grieves, He hurts and feels rejected and unloved. We treat Him the same way we treat others. God experienced the hurt and pain of leaving His son in the hands of a wicked and sinful generation. But He did not do it selfishly so we would love Him but for us to gain eternal life with Him, knowing that without His help we would be condemned to eternal punishment. What a wonderful God.

Then, why do some of us behave the way we do? Why can't we see that obeying God is better than life? Throughout the Bible there are instructions and illustrations as to how to become more obedient, yet we fall in the same predicament as those who chose to disobey. I pray that we would all desire to heed to the advice of those who have gone before us and have come through as fine gold. God told Solomon in a dream, "If you walk in My ways, to keep My statues and My commandments, as your father David walked, then I will lengthen your days" (1 kings 3:14, NKJV) "For this is the love of God, that we keep His commandments. And His commandments are not burdensome" (1 John 5: 3, NKJV).

In the end I stand with Peter and the other apostles who answered their accusers, "We ought to obey God rather than men" (Acts 5:29, NKJV).

Personal Reflection

_____

_____

_____

_____

_____

_____

_____

_____

_____

_____

_____

_____

_____

_____

_____

_____

_____

_____

_____

_____

_____

_____

_____

Chapter 5

I Am the God Who Heals You

"But He was wounded for our transgressions,
He was bruised for our iniquities; the
chastisement for our peace was upon Him,
and by His stripes we are healed"
(Isaiah 53:5, NKJV).

The world appears to be in chaos in fact most people say they have never seen it so badly disarrayed. I decided to talk to some of the older folks to hear what they had to say about growing up in their generation. I was thrilled to hear their stories and how they survived. As they tell their stories about the times when they were children, their stories all sounded very similar. They reflected on the times when parents could not find a job or how they could barely find food or when they couldn't go to the doctor because they could not afford the medical bill. Today, for some of us, the stories are the same. I guess it is our time to learn from the experiences of the older generation as to how they made it this far.

When God created the heavens and the earth everything was good. Then Satan deceived man and man sinned. But it didn't stop there, for when man chose to obey Satan rather than God he decided who would rule over him on earth. Satan was given the power by God along with the rest of the evil angels to roam the earth and rule over its people. The earth was devastated because of sin. The trees died, the grass withered, animals became vicious and were no longer man's friend. Sin made us enemies with our fellow man and with the God who created us.

Let's think about it. Look at the way we live today. Why is it that most of us only say "hi" to our neighbors but we never stop to have a conversation? The people we see every day at work don't even come over for dinner because some of us are afraid of how everything will turn out. Some of us are afraid of being judged by our peers or more than anything we are afraid to trust anyone. Let's face it; opening up our hearts to others is quite a risk. We rarely take a chance to give a piece of our self to someone for fear they will prove to be unfaithful. And so it is with almost all our relationships. We keep everything within the family, that way, we remain safe and untouchable. No one will be able to judge us. After all, they are all hateful, resentful, covetous people who want only one thing and that is to come into our lives, get to know us and then hurt us.

Sad to say, many of us have been hurt so many times by those we have allowed to enter into our lives that we develop a fear of building new and lasting relationships. Maybe this is what you are going through at this time and it hurts. The plain truth is it becomes lonely when there is no one to confide in or a shoulder to lean on when times get hard. Keeping it safe doesn't always work out for the best. We may gain our privacy in protecting ourselves but we miss out on the opportunity of making a difference in the life of another human being.

As I reflect on my own hurts and challenges over the years I am reminded of the story of Job. He was a wealthy man, a man who loved the Lord and walked in His statues. God loved Job therefore He blessed Him tremendously. Job had a fine wife and many good-looking children. He prospered in his business and had many servants and friends, and he was obedient to God's will. God was very proud of Job and Satan knew it. You see, God would let Satan know that there were still hope for mankind to make it back to His kingdom, and that man was still able to live blameless and upright in spite of the evil that surrounded them. Job was God's living proof that this was possible but Satan could not be content with God's happiness for his heart's desire was to hurt God. So Satan tried to use his tactics on the Creator of the universe. "Oh yah, you know he only fear You because of what You can give him. You have placed a fence around Job and his family but I dare you to move that protection and see if Job will still love and worship you". It didn't take God long to think about Satan's request because He knew Job's heart and trusted Job's love for Him. God's one request was that Satan would not take Job's life. Of course Satan left feeling he had won the challenge already.

When I think about the discussion God had with Satan in the presence of everyone at that meeting, I questioned my walk with God and wondered if He feels the same about me the way He felt about Job. Do I make Him proud and can He brag about me? I may never know, but there is one thing I do know, He loves me and He wants me to succeed. Satan couldn't wait to start proving to God that he was right about Job. So he destroyed Job's children, his animals, his servants. Everything that Job had loved and worked to attain was taken away. The losses were too much, yet in all of Job's hurt and pain he cried out, "Naked I came from my mother's womb, and naked I shall return there. The lord gave, and the Lord has taken away; blessed be the name of the Lord. In all this, Job did not sin nor charge God with wrong" (Job 1:21& 22, NKJV).

The story did not stop there, for though Satan wanted to force Job to curse and deny the very God who made him, he stood firm. Satan tried in every way to defeat Job. He even sent Job's wife to encourage him to curse God and die and as if that weren't enough, he sent Job's friends to judge and condemn him. When life gets rough and hard that is when you know your true friends.

After losing my job in 2009, I felt abandoned by people I had called my friends. I would go to church and hoped that someone would asked me how I was making it or is there any way I can help but instead they were cold towards me. These are some of the very people I had helped in the past and prayed and cried with. I was in church one morning and was seated next to a friend who knew my predicament. I was hurting so much so I asked, "Have you ever prayed for me". She answered me so sternly, "Have you ever asked me to pray for you?" I was so shocked I could not respond. When does someone have to ask a friend to pray for them? I thought that was natural for brethren to do when they know one of the flocks was hurting. Maybe I had this praying thing all wrong for I have been praying for people who I knew needed an extra blessing from God. Maybe my friend was going through her own situation at the time so I prayed that God would bless her and her family, and while He is blessing her to bless me as well. Satan's aim is to discourage Christians to lose their faith, and he will use even a friend.

Job's friends came to pray, but they also came to condemn. No wonder people are so afraid to have friends. It is human nature to do wrong towards his fellow man, so why should we think a friend would not disappoint us? Haven't we disappointed them? We all make mistakes and we have to be willing to forgive and to let go. Job's friends got a dose of their own medicine when God healed Job and restored his blessing. But remember, if it were not for Job's prayer over his friends and their request for forgiveness, they would be wiped off from the face of the earth. In the end God used these same friends and Job's acquaintances to help him back on his feet. Remember, they came bearing gifts; therefore, Job became twice as rich.

When you walk in the way of the Lord He will use the very people that cursed you to bless you. Sometimes when life gives us a hard blow we feel like giving up. We cry and pray and pray and cry yet our prayers seemingly go unanswered. Has God forgotten us or is He even there? Is He concerned with our problems and our burdens? Why do the wicked seem to always prosper? In anguish we cry out, "When will God restore joy and gladness to my life? When I take one step forward, circumstances cause me to take ten steps back. Please draw near dear Lord, as your child cries out for your help!" Our experience maybe different but our hurt and pain are the same. But listen to me carefully. You can't give up! For it is when you are at the weakest point of your life that God comes shining through. Yes, He has proven this over and over and over again. For His word said, "And the Lord will make you the head and not the tail; you shall be above only, and not be beneath, if you heed the commandments of the lord your God, which I command you today, and are careful to observe them" (Deuteronomy 28:13, NKJV).

The woman with the issue of blood had been struggling with her infirmity for years. She had heard about Jesus and the great miracles that He had worked. She heard that sometimes just by a touch from His hand the blind would see and the lame would walk. She heard that sometimes all Jesus had to do was to give a word. Then she saw the crowd and someone shouted, "It is Jesus. He is here in our own city". I bet she had gone over in her mind time and time again how she would approach Jesus and ask Him to do just this one thing. Now Jesus was here, she couldn't see Him but she could hear Him. "But there is a crowd! How am I going to get to Him?" She wondered, "He is the only one who can restore my body. Please God, help me. The crowd is too thick. Oh God of Abraham, Isaac and Jacob, hear my cry! I only want to touch your son for there is no hope that I will even get to talk with Him. Lord God, just give me the strength to touch Him, for if I just touch a piece of His clothing I will be healed."

As she pushed through the crowd, the crowd pushed back. But her determination would not let her quit. She fell but she got back up again even more determined to get to Jesus. Then suddenly she touched Him. It was not much of a touch for it was only a piece of Jesus' clothing. "But I touched Him! I touched Him! Thank You God!" Then, she felt a change in her body, for suddenly that continued flowing of blood stopped and it was as if her whole body became alive again. Her strength was made new. "Could it be I am healed? Yes, I am healed! Thank You God!" Then someone spoke within the crowd, "Who touched Me? Who touched Me?" Her heart began beating faster and faster for Jesus was looking straight at her and she at Him. She fell down at Jesus' feet and confessed her story. Then Jesus said to her, "Daughter, your faith has made you well. Go in peace, and be healed of your affliction" (Mark 5:34, NKJV).

Apart from the amazing fact that her faith in God healed her, she got to speak to Jesus in spite of the crowd. Although there were so many people, Jesus the son of God, took the time to address her personally. God is the only one who can heal us. Whether it is sickness, addictions, finances, God can heal your situation. If you are jobless, homeless, or heartless, God can meet you just as you are. He wants to heal you and me. He wants to restore what was taken from us by Satan. All He asks of us is to be obedient to His commandments and to keep our eyes fixed on Him. Job was afflicted even though he was a child of God, but he never gave up hope. There are many other examples in the Word of God about God's healing powers and His mercies. There are even people around you who can testify to the fact that God continues to heal even today. I am sure He has even moved in your own life. I do believe that I am blessed and God is going to pour out an extra blessing over my life. God is ready to do the same for you and your loved ones because He is the God who heals.

Personal Reflection

_____

_____

_____

_____

_____

_____

_____

_____

_____

_____

_____

_____

_____

_____

_____

_____

_____

_____

_____

_____

_____

_____

_____

_____

_____

_____

Chapter 6

I Would Never Leave You Comfortless

"Blessed be the God and Father of our Lord Jesus Christ, the Father of mercies and God of all comfort; who comforts us in all our tribulation, that we may be able to comfort those who are in any trouble, with the comfort with which we ourselves are comforted by God. For as the sufferings of Christ abound in us, so our consolation also abound through Christ"
(2 Corinthians 1:3-5, NKJV).

Sometimes in life we get discouraged because of situations and circumstances that appear as though they would overcome us. Many of us are trapped in those circumstances and feel like there is no escape. But friends, I want to let you know today that there is a way out; God is everywhere and there is nothing under the sun that He does not see and hear; there is nothing He does not understand. God can release the bondage that seems to weigh you down; He can break the chains that have enslaved you for so long. My friends, God is in the miracle working business! He wants to show you how He can make the impossible possible. He has done it for me and He can do it for you. God has never stopped performing the impossible. He wants to free you because He loves you. He wants to comfort you.

We have all experienced things in life that somehow pushes us to become a better person or hinders us from moving forward. My most challenging experience started the day I was conceived. Although I had nothing to do with my conception God had already ordained a plan for my life. I have always believed that I was conceived in love even though my mother and father were teenagers at the time, and having a child out of wedlock in those days were similar to blasphemy. My father had moved on with his life and started a family of his own while my mother, with the help of her parents, raised, loved, and nurtured me. For years I felt rejected by my father and his family, yet I didn't want to believe it; after all, he would call me once in a while just to find out if I was "ok". Later, as I grew older and started a family of my own, my dad become a Santa Clause to my children as he would send a post card with a check to buy gifts to place under the Christmas tree once a year. However my dad chose to show his love for me was ok; it did not matter what he did but that he did. After all, some children have never seen their dad/mom or even know if he/she exists. I knew where my dad was and knowing that he gave me some attention, however small, was enough to prove that he loved me. For years I had called him father and done everything a daughter could do to feel loved and accepted. I thought that if I gave love it would come right back to me. Then, just when I felt certain of my father's love, all Hell broke lose.

I was 40 years old when I received the phone call that my father didn't really love me and that I needed to do a paternity test for my father to prove that I was his own. I was in shock! My world as I knew it was falling apart. Although I didn't have the unconditional love of a father, at least I had something. I had no doubt that my dad was my biological father, we looked too much alike. What concerned me most was how my children would be affected. I have two wonderful daughters and I wanted to protect them as much as possible. My husband was very supportive and tried to comfort me in every way but I could not be comforted. I cried for days. Later I had to seek therapy as I went through a mild depression.

My father requested that I take a DNA test which proved to be 99.99999 percent positive. I am my father's daughter. However, did it improve our relationship? No it did not. In my opinion, it made me see the true heart of my father towards me. My father put a price tag on his love for me. The DNA was now the only proof for acceptance; not withstanding the fact that he had already invested over 30 years into our father-daughter relationship.

There are so many children who are born without knowing the love of a father. There are millions in our country and all over the world who still long for the love of a father even though they are in their late stages of life. They yearn to hear the words, "I am sorry for not being a good father to you my child". Many fatherless children become so troubled in life they end up being addicts, criminals, or even end up abusing their own children. Statistic shows, fathers who were deserted as children are sometimes fearful of repeating their father's mistake, and sadly most of them do.

Even after the death of an absentee father many children go on yearning for their love. I remember talking to an elderly man who had lost his wife and was in the early stage of grieving. While reflecting on his life and his experience with death he remembered his father's death. He started to cry uncontrollably. When he had calmed down, I asked how it was for him at the time of his father's passing. The man began venting hurtful things about his father. He ended up cursing his father for the life he had forced his family to live. My heart began to break—it had hit home. A father has the power to make or break a child; mothers do as well, but even more so a father. How sad it was to see a man in his late 70's crying for the love of his father who was already in the grave. My only advice for him was to forgive his father so he could move on with his grief. I advised him to go to his father's graveside and state all he had in his heart towards him, so he did. I saw him several times after that and he would always thank me for my suggestion to make reconciliation and for helping him to properly close that chapter of his life. This elderly man, though grieving the loss of his wife was able to move on after years of being tormented by the mistakes of his father.

In my own way I thanked the person at the other end of the phone for revealing the reason for the disconnection between my father and me. It was better to speak the truth than to pretend the truth. I had always felt that the air wasn't sincere when we would come together, so it is safe to say the air was cleared. Since then things did change for all the families involved. After much therapy, we made peace. Being able to forgive has helped me move on and when Christ becomes your whole life, love becomes easy to live. I continue to love and will forever love my father.

In spite of all the heartache and pain over the years, I am always comforted by the love of Christ. He has given me a wonderful husband and two wonderful daughters, not to mention a mother who loves and cares for me deeply. My mother, as a single woman, made many sacrifices to care for her children. I may not have had the legacy of having a father in the home but we experienced love. As a grown woman and now a mother myself, I appreciate my mother even more. There is nothing she wouldn't do to help her children and her family. Now that my grandparents have past away she is the glue that holds us all together. Through my father's family I have also felt God's embrace. My aunts and uncle and their families never made me feel unloved. I was blessed with the privilege of having my paternal grandmother shower her love on me and lay hands on my children and blessed them before she died. God gave me the comfort in knowing that though I may not have the unconditional love of an earthly father, I am loved by a heavenly Father. Thank you Father God.

We all suffer under different circumstances in life. For some it may be the death of a loved one or the loss of a long relationship, a divorce, a job, a home, or a financial or health situation. The only thing that maters right now is that you are hurting and that your heart is broken. Why not ask God to comfort you today, right now. He wants to comfort you as a father should comfort his children. For He is a compassionate father as seen in Luke 7:13, (NKJV). He is a merciful God. "Blessed be the God and Father of our Lord Jesus Christ, the father of mercies and God of all comfort; who comforts us in all our tribulations, that we may be able to comfort those who are in any trouble, with the comfort with which we ourselves are comforted by God" (2 Corinthians 1:3&4, NKJV).

Following Christ's death and burial, His disciples were very worried. They had walked with Jesus for approximately three years and have seen Him work many miracles. He could have taken Himself off the cross if He wanted to, but He didn't. The disciples were distraught with fear. What will happen to them now that Jesus was no longer with them? In the past they could always depend on Jesus to comfort them when they were down; He knew just how to fix any situation. Some must have thought to go back to their previous occupation and just carry on with their lives. But then Jesus stepped in once again. In their hurt and brokenness they had forgotten the promise Jesus had made to them. He said, "Destroy this temple, and in three days I will raise it up" (John 2: 19 NKJV). Many of them did not understand then, but after His death it was revealed to them. Jesus had returned to comfort them in their grief and sorrow. He had made an appearance to the women who came to care for His dead body and now He must reveal Himself to His disciples. So the command was given, "Go tell His disciples and Peter that He is going before you into Galilee; there you will see Him, as He said to you" (Mark 16:7, NKJV). How swift must have been the footsteps of those women and how happy they must have been to carry the good news to the disciples, especially to Peter? Sadly no one believed them. The disciples had to return to the grave to see the proof for themselves. Jesus is alive! He is risen from the dead! How victorious and amazing are the sound of those words. "Jesus Christ our Savior is alive!" They had seen Him for themselves and spent time together with Him. They finally understood the meaning of every word spoken before by the Lord. It all made sense to them now. The body is only temporary. Life on earth is but for a moment. Only with Christ in your heart can you live forever. Yes, it all made sense. Jesus is the living proof.

Now Jesus would meet with them one last time for He was leaving. But this time they had no fear because He had given them specific instructions to stay in Jerusalem until they received Power from on high. It was the promise of the Holy Spirit, The Comforter. Jesus explained, "It is to your advantage that I go away; for if I do not go away, the Helper will not come to you; but if I depart I will send Him to you" (John 16: 7, NKJV). He also specifies what will happen when the comforter comes. "And when He has come, He will convict the world of sin, and of righteousness, and of judgment: of sin, because they do not believe in Me; of righteousness, because I go to My Father and you see Me no more; of judgment, because the ruler of this world is judged" (John 16:8-11, NKJV). Jesus said He would never leave us comfortless. He wants to be a part of our lives and our daily experiences. We only have to let Him. He didn't promise that there would be no pain or sorrow; He promised to hold our hands all the way through if we will let Him.

That's the secret of the Christian believers: they keep smiling even when they should be crying, they have joy even when they should be sad. It is amazing to see a Christian family, though experiencing death, the joy they possess knowing they will see their loved one in the resurrection. The word of God said we will all be resurrected when Christ breaks through the bar of Heaven. "For the Lord Himself will descend from Heaven with a shout, with the voice of an archangel, and with the trumpet of God. And the dead in Christ will rise first. Then we who are alive and remain shall be caught up together with them in the clouds to meet the Lord in the air. And thus we shall always be with the Lord. Therefore comfort one another with these words" (1Thessalonians 4: 16-18, NKJV).

Yes, Heaven is real and so is Hell. It is so wonderful to know that we still have time to make a choice. We can either follow Christ and receive eternal life or follow the prince of this world, Satan and receive eternal damnation. There is no time for excuses! Life is too short and it quickly slips away. While the Spirit of God is speaking to your heart, listen for He cares about you. The only thing that makes the difference is the choice you will make right now. Jesus made His choice for you and me when He went to Calvary. He is waiting to comfort you at this very moment. You can kneel by your bed or bow your head wherever you are right now. Ask Him to come into your heart. He is waiting to give you true joy and comfort if you will let Him.

There is nothing you can do to cause God to stop caring for you! For even when God is angry with you, He still provides comfort. His anger is only for a moment. The prophet Isaiah said, "O Lord, I will praise You; though You were angry with me, Your anger is turned away and you comfort me" (Isaiah 12:1, NKJV). God wants to heal you, but you have to do your part. He wants you to repent from your sins. He wants you to empty yourself of all the lies, hatefulness, and resentment; He wants you to give Him all your sin. God wants to set you free, but first you have to ask for His help. He cannot do it without your permission for He is a gentle Lamb. He wants us to live a holy and healthy life. Jesus is a balm in Gilead. He will make His people whole again. Jesus promised, "They shall neither hunger anymore nor thirst anymore; the sun shall not strike them, nor any heat; for the Lamb who is in the midst of the throne will shepherd them and lead them to living fountains of waters. And God will wipe away every tear from their eyes" (Revelation 7:16 &17, NKJV). *He is my only Comfort.* Why don't you let Him be your Comfort today?

Personal Reflection

Chapter 7

Prove Me Now

"Bring all the tithes into the storehouse, that there may be food in my house, and try Me now in this" says the Lord of host, "if I will not open for you the windows of Heaven and pour out for you such blessing that there will not be room enough to receive it"
(Malachi 3:10, NKJV).

Time after time God has proven Himself to me and yet sometimes when I'm faced with difficult problems, they seems so hard to bear and I lose courage. Has that ever happened to you? It was the beginning of the year 2009 when I found out that I among others might be terminated from my job. The economy was quickly falling into a recession and all businesses had an impact on each other and mine was no exception. Everyone was affected, not just in America but all over the world. At first, I thought about how losing my job would affect my family, and what I could do to sustain my finances so it would take me through the difficult times ahead. 'I am ready for anything", I said. "God promised He would take care of me, and He will, because He has never broken a promise."

The time came for my termination. I was prepared and my heart rejoiced for I knew God was in total control. I felt a certain peace within me for I knew it was time for me to move on. God had other plans for my life. I was ready for what ever God had decided for me to do. More than ever, I felt as though God was in total control. For every month that followed my termination I saw how God moved in my life and provided for me and my family. My bills were paid on time and my needs met. It was then God laid on my heart the desire to finish a promise that I had made to Him almost three years prior, and that was to finish this book.

Approximately three years ago I felt impressed by the Holy Spirit to write about the things that affected us most on the inside. The fact is we never talk about our true feelings to others. Most of us have secret thoughts and ideas and some are even possessed with demons that affect our relationship with God. I wanted to share my experiences with others, mostly young people, so that they could be encouraged on their Christian journey. Through Devine inspiration I was impressed to entitle my book, The Invisible "me". Each time that I would write a few pages I would allow days and weeks to pass before returning to my computer to finish my book assignment. This went on for two years. I felt guilty at times because I knew I was being disobedient to God. I remember one day when I felt so impressed to write, I got on the computer and I must have written four or five pages. I felt pleased, for finally I was getting somewhere. Suddenly everything on the screen went blank. I could not retrieve my manuscript. All the pages I had written previously, along with the five new pages, were gone. They had disappeared.

The job of retrieving the file was too complicated for me so I took my laptop to the experts. They could not find my file anywhere. How could it have disappeared when I had spent months putting my thoughts on paper? After all, I was doing what God had asked me to do. I was being obedient so why did this happen to me? I was depressed for weeks and thought God had abandoned me. At the time I had talked with my pastor and his advice was to start over. Start over! Was that all the advice he could give me? Was he aware of all the time I had put into this thing and all the great ideas I had lost. I then turned my anger toward God. God could have protected my manuscript but He allowed Satan to destroy it. Isn't it odd how we always seem to blame someone else for our mistakes without taking responsibility for the part we play in the matter? And how is it Satan's fault? I think we give him way too much credit than he deserves. I should have taken precaution to save my file. I did not. Could it be that God wanted to reveal something to me within this test?

It was later that the Holy Spirit revealed what had happened. You see, "The Invisible me" was not about "me" but about an all-knowing, all-loving yet invisible God. He is the Invisible "ME". He wanted me to capture His invisibility in the life of men. The Invisible God is in deed visible in my life and in yours. God wants to have a relationship with us. We make ourselves so busy that we can hardly find time to pray much less to read His words. Since I lost my job I have spent more time in His word than ever before. He had taken away my job, the thing that kept me so busy, so that I could focus on Him. He has given me all the time in the world to focus on this book and to build a better relationship with Him while providing for my needs.

God does not make mistakes. He allows disappointments and tribulations in our lives so we can prove Him. Satan tests us and so does God. This battle that we are in is a spiritual one. His word said, "For we wrestle not against flesh and blood, but against principalities, against powers, against the rulers of darkness of this world, against spiritual wickedness in high places (Ephesians 6:12, KJV). Every day we wake up it is a new day to prove God. He is faithful. When He said, He will not leave us nor forsake us, He means it. Sometimes we feel as though we are alone, but like footprints in the sand, God carries us in His arms when we can't go on.

Time after time we get disappointed with our own lives. "My marriage failed." "My children have left the church". "I am a financial wreck". "I will never get a promotion". "My life is a complete failure". It is always something new. You may ask, "When will I ever be able to enjoy the good life or when will I ever be happy?" I want you to know that "the good life" only last for but a moment, true joy last for eternity.

Think about it. When Jesus was on earth He lived a very difficult life. In the end He was put to death. If Jesus is our example for walking this Christian path, how then can we keep seeking for anything more? Please do not get me wrong. It is ok to have a nice house, drive a nice car, and make good money even become a millionaire, but remember having all these things do not mean you will not continue to have trials and tribulations. The millionaire, for instance, has to make sure he keeps his eye on his wealth. He may have problems trusting his friends and family members in regards to their motives towards him and his money. Then there is the death issue of who will get his millions after he dies. No wonder so many millionaires leave their money to charity or to their pets instead of their own family.

Jesus is the example of what true joy looks like. The word of God says, "Looking unto Jesus, the author and finisher of our faith, who for the joy that was set before Him endured the cross, despising the shame, and has sat down at the right hand of the throne of God. For consider Him who endured such hostility from sinners against Himself, lest you become weary and discouraged in your souls" (Hebrew 12:2, 3, NKJV). What a wonderful Lord. His joy comes from knowing at the end of His suffering He would overcome the hold that Satan has on our lives, for He came to redeem us for Himself so that we too would finally glory in His joy. The word of God gives us healing, joy and insight in times of discouragement. Jeremiah had proven it time and time again. He said, "Your words were found, and I ate them, and Your word was to me the joy and rejoicing of my heart; for I am called by your name, O Lord God of hosts" (Jeremiah 15: 16, NKJV).

True joy comes through obedience to the will of Christ. The Christian should count it all joy to be obedient to our Lord and Savior. If we notice throughout both the Old and New Testament, God implores us to be obedient. He said if you are obedient, in other words, if you do what I have commanded you to do then you will gain the joy that only I can give. From my own experience, I find that when I get myself into trouble I am mostly out of the will of Christ. Every Christian knows when he or she is being disobedient to God. I know because the Holy Spirit convicts me. I thought about Jonah and how he willfully tried to do his own thing after God gave him specific instructions about Nineveh. Jonah soon found out that when God says go He means it. I also thought about Moses and the children of Israel in the wilderness. It took them forty years to reach the promise land although it was in plain site. God had to test their obedience. Almost all the people who came from Egypt died except a few obedient ones. Moses was unable to see the promise land because he did not follow God's instructions. Think about Naaman the leper in the New Testament. The prophet of the Lord told him to go dip himself seven times in the Jordon, the dirtiest river, so he would be cleansed of his leprosy. Not until he followed the instruction, could he receive healing from his disease. I am sure he must have felt the joy that God gives to all who obey him.

God wants us to prove Him in everything. He wants to be so much a part of our lives. God wants us to prove Him in all the plans we make for our lives. We cannot do it all on our own. We need direction from the greatest designer of all times. He wants us to prove Him in our relationships, in our education, and in our marriages. He wants us to prove Him in times of health and in times of sickness. God wants us to prove Him in our business and our finances. The prophet Malachi proclaims the word of God. He said, "'Bring all the tithes into the storehouse, that there may be food in my house, and try Me now in this' says the Lord of host, 'if I will not open for you the windows of Heaven and pour out for you such blessing that there will not be room enough to receive it'" (Malachi 3:10, NKJV).

What are you waiting for? Turn your situation over to Him and try Him today. He said in His words; "casting all your care upon Him, for He cares for you" (1Peter 5:7, NKJV). It does not matter what you have done in your life. God is only interested in you. He is at your heart's door knocking, waiting for you to open your heart and let Him in. I gave my life to Christ Jesus at the age of eleven. I may not have always followed His rules, but He knows my heart and He knows that I love Him, so like a parent He gently scolds me to get me back on tract. I am sure that you too have proven His love. He has given all of us another day to repent of our sins. For God is patient. But patience has its limits. As in the days of Noah, Sodom and Gomorrah and Israel in the wilderness, God has proven that He will not always strive with man. He is God and He is worthy of our praise. It is He who created us into living beings. He blew breath into our nostrils and without Him we would certainly die. He loves us, but He also wants us to love Him. He is at this time, waiting with open arms to receive us and to pour out blessings after blessing upon us. Why don't you take Him at His word and prove Him today? For God is not slack concerning His promise. I can testify. The Invisible "ME" has never failed.

Personal Reflection

_____

_____

_____

_____

_____

_____

_____

_____

_____

_____

_____

_____

_____

_____

_____

_____

_____

_____

_____

_____

_____

_____

_____

_____

_____

The Invisible Me Bible References

❖ I Am Who I AM .... The Lord God of your fathers, the God of Abraham, the God of Isaac, and the God of Jacob, has sent me to you. This is my name forever, and this is My memorial to all generations. (Exodus 3:14&15, NKJV).

❖ Ask and it will be given to you; seek, and you will find; knock, and it will be opened to you. (Mathew 7:7, NKJV).

❖ For I know the thoughts that I think toward you, says the Lord, thoughts of peace and not of evil, to give you a future and a hope. Then you will call upon Me and go and pray to Me, and I will listen to you; and you will seek Me and find Me, when you search for Me with all your heart (Jeremiah 29:11-13, NKJV).

❖ You are the God who Sees for she said, "Have I also here seen Him who sees me?" (Genesis 16:13, NKJV).

❖ Take careful heed to yourselves, for you saw no form when the Lord spoke to you at Horeb out of the midst of the fire, lest you act corruptly and make yourselves a carved image in the form of any figure: the likeness of male or female, the likeness of any animal that is on the earth or the likeness of any winged bird that flies in the air, the likeness of anything that creeps on the ground or the likeness of any fish that is in the water beneath the earth. And take heed, lest you lift your eyes to heaven, and when you see the sun, the moon, and the stars, all the host of heaven, you feel driven to worship them and serve them, which the Lord your God has given to all peoples under the whole heaven as a heritage (Deuteronomy 4 :15-19, NKJV).

❖ "I Am Who I Am." And He said, 'Thus you shall say to the children of Israel, 'I AM has sent me to you'" (Exodus 3:14, NKJV).

❖ "I am One who bears witness of Myself, and the Father who sent Me bears witness of Me" (John 8:18, NKJV).

❖ "You are from beneath; I am from above. You are of this world; I am not of this world" (John 8:23, NKJV)

❖ "Most assuredly, I say to you, before Abraham was, I AM" (John 8:58, NKJV).

❖ For the Lord does not see as man sees; for man looks at the outward appearance, but the Lord looks at the heart (1 Samuel 16: 7, NKJV).

❖ Therefore humble yourselves under the mighty hand of God, that He may exalt you in due time, casting all your care upon Him, for He cares for you (1 Peter 5:6&7, NKJV).

❖ "What have you done? The voice of your brother's blood cries out to Me from the ground" (Genesis 4:10, NKJV).

❖ "Why are you angry? And why has your countenance fallen? If you do well, will you not be accepted? And if you do not do well, sin lies at the door. And its desire is for you, but you should rule over it" (Genesis 4:6&7, NKJV).

❖ "My punishment is greater than I can bear! Surely You have driven me out this day from the face of the ground; I shall be hidden from Your face; I shall be a fugitive and a vagabond on the earth, and it will happen that anyone who finds me will kill me" (Genesis 4:13&14, NKJV).

❖ "Whoever kills Cain, vengeance shall be taken on him sevenfold" (Genesis 4:15, NKJV).

❖ For the wages of sin is death, but the gift of God is eternal life in Christ Jesus our Lord (Romans 6:23, NKJV).

❖ "Fear not, for I am with you. Be not dismayed, for I am your God. I will strengthen you, yes

I will help you; I will uphold you with my righteous right hand" (Isaiah 41: 10, NKJV).

❖ Trust in the Lord, and do good. Dwell in the land, and feed on His faithfulness. Delight yourself also in the Lord, and He shall give you the desires of your heart (Psalm 37: 3 &4, NKJV).

❖ "Of every tree of the garden you may freely eat; but of the tree of the knowledge of good and evil you shall not eat, for in the day that you eat of it you shall surely die" (Geneses 2: 16 &17, NKJV).

❖ Then the serpent said to the woman, "You will not surely die" (Genesis 3:4, NKJV).

❖ And they heard the sound of the Lord God walking in the garden in the cool of the day, Adam and his wife hid themselves from the present of the Lord God among the trees of the garden (Geneses 3:8, NKJV).

❖ "O My Father, if it is possible, let this cup pass from Me; nevertheless, not as I will, but as You will" (Matthew 26:42, NKJV).

❖ "My God, My God, why have You forsaken Me?" (Matthew 27:46, NKJV).

❖ Then the sun was darkened, and the veil of the temple was torn in two. And when Jesus had cried out with a loud voice, He said, 'Father into your hands I commit My spirit.' Having said this, He breathed His last (Luke 23:45-46, NKJV).

❖ Who shall separate us from the love of Christ? Shall tribulation, or distress, or persecution, or famine, or nakedness, or peril, or sword? As it is written; 'for Your sake we are killed all day long; We are accounted as sheep for the slaughter.' Yet in all these things we are more than conquerors through Him who loved us. For I am persuaded that neither death nor life, nor angels nor principalities nor powers, nor things present nor things to come, nor height nor depth, nor any other created thing, shall be able to separate us from the love of God which is in Christ Jesus our Lord (Romans 8:35-39, NKJV).

❖ "If you love Me, keep My commandments" (John 14:15, NKJV).

❖ And Abraham stretched out his hand and took the knife to slay his son. But the angel of the Lord called to him from heaven and said, 'Abraham, Abraham!' So he said, 'Here I am.' And He said, 'Do not lay your hand on the lad, or do anything to him; for now I know that you fear God, since you have not withheld your son, your only son, from Me'(Genesis 22: 10, 11&12, NKJV).

❖ "By Myself I have sworn, because you have done this thing, and have not withheld your son, your only son, blessing I will bless you and multiplying I will multiply your descendants as the stars of the heaven and as the sand which is on the seashore; and your descendants shall possess the gate of their enemies. In your seed all the nations of the earth shall be blessed, because you have obeyed My voice" (Geneses 22: 16-18, NKJV).

❖ "If you walk in My ways, to keep My statues and My commandments, as your father David walked, then I will lengthen your days" (1 kings 3:14, NKJV).

- ❖ For this is the love of God, that we keep His commandments. And His commandments are not burdensome (1 John 5: 3, NKJV).

- ❖ We ought to obey God rather than men (Acts 5:29, NKJV).

- ❖ But He was wounded for our transgressions, He was bruised for our iniquities; the chastisement for our peace was upon Him, and by His stripes we are healed (Isaiah 53:5, NKJV).

- ❖ "Naked I came from my mother's womb, and naked I shall return there. The lord gave, and the Lord has taken away; blessed be the name of the Lord". In all this, Job did not sin nor charge God with wrong (Job 1:21& 22, NKJV).

- ❖ And the Lord will make you the head and not the tail; you shall be above only, and not be beneath, if you heed the commandments of the lord your God, which I command you today, and are careful to observe them" (Deuteronomy 28:13, NKJV).

❖ "Daughter, your faith has made you well. Go in peace, and be heal of your afflictions" (Mark 5:34, NKJV).

❖ "Blessed be the God and Father of our Lord Jesus Christ, the Father of mercies and God of all comfort; who comforts us in all our tribulation that we may be able to comfort those who are in any trouble, with the comfort with which we ourselves are comforted by God. For as the sufferings of Christ abound in us, so our consolation also abound through Christ" (2 Corinthians 1:3-5, NKJV).

❖ When the Lord saw her, He had compassion on her, "Do not weep" (Luke 7:13, NKJV).

❖ "Go tell His disciples and Peter that He is going before you into Galilee; there you will see Him, as He said to you" (Mark 16:7, NKJV).

❖ Jesus explained, It is to your advantage that I go away; for if I do not go away, the Helper will not come to you; but if I depart

I will send Him to you". "And when He comes, He will convict the world of sin, and of righteousness and of judgment: of sin, because they do not believe in Me; of righteousness, because I go to My Father and you see Me no more; of judgment, because the ruler of this world is judged" (John 16:7-11, NKJV).

❖ For the Lord Himself will descend from heaven with a shout, with the voice of an archangel, and with the trumpet of God. And the dead in Christ will rise first. Then we who are alive and remain shall be caught up together with them in the clouds to meet the Lord in the air. And thus we shall always be with the Lord. Therefore comfort one another with these words (1Thessalonians 4: 16-18, NKJV).

❖ David said, "O Lord, I will praise You; though You were angry with me, Your anger is turned away and you comfort me" (Isaiah 12:1, NKJV).

❖ They shall neither hunger anymore nor thirst anymore; the sun shall not strike them, nor any heat; for the Lamb who is in the midst of the throne will shepherd them and lead them to living fountains of waters. And God will wipe away every tear from their eyes (Revelation 7:16 &17, NKJV).

❖ "Bring all the tithes into the storehouse, that there may be food in my house, and try Me now in this" says the Lord of host, "if I will not open for you the windows of heaven and pour out for you such blessing that there will not be room enough to receive it" (Malachi 3:10, NKJV).

❖ For we wrestle not against flesh and blood, but against principalities, against powers, against the rulers of darkness of this world, against spiritual wickedness in high places (Ephesians 6:12, KJV).

❖ Looking unto Jesus, the author and finisher of our faith, who for the joy that was set before Him endured the cross, despising the shame, and has sat down at the right hand of the throne of God. For consider Him who endured such hostility from sinners against Himself, lest you become weary and discouraged in your souls (Hebrew 12:2, 3, NKJV).

❖   Your words were found, and I ate them, and Your word was to me the joy and rejoicing of my heart; for I am called by your name, O Lord God of hosts (Jeremiah 15: 16, NKJV).